GOD'S TEMPLATE FOR YOU MARRIAGE; *Biblical ways for a Christ-centered marriage*

Jefferson Hills

Table of Contents

Chapter One

THE ORIGIN OF MARRIAGE

Hebrew Scripture

According to Sacred Scripture, God coordinated marriage as the peak of creation. On the sixth day, in the foremost creation story, the Book of Genesis tells us: "God made man in his image; in the magnificent picture he made him; male and female he made them. God inclined toward them, saying: 'Be rich and copy, fill the earth and curb it'" (Genesis 1: 27-28).

God says "it isn't perfect for a man to be isolated from every other person in the second creation story, that. I will make a sensible accessory for him." (Genesis 2:18). This sensible accomplice was outlined from the genuine rib of man and appropriately woman was "tissue of his tissue" (Genesis 2:22-23).

Woman, then, is man's identical in honorability and the one closest to his heart. Since man and woman were made for one another, "a man passes on his father and mother and holds to his soul mate, and the two of them become one tissue" (Genesis 2: 24). Consecrated text educates that marriage is surely not a straightforward human association, but something God spread out from the supporting of world.

Sin accomplished a break with God, yet it in like manner burst the principal cooperation among man and woman. Adam and Eve blamed everyone something else for what had happened and were as of now embarrassed by their exposed state (Genesis 3:7-13). The Old Testament shows how sin affected the conventionality of marriage. There is the polygamy of the patriarchs and rulers. Moses allowed independence because of people's "savagery" (see Deuteronomy 24:1 and Matthew 19:8). Individuals didn't treat each other with uprightness, honor, and love as God had anticipated. In any case, while bad behavior mutilated the respectability of marriage, it didn't obliterate it.

New Testament

Christians are new signs in Christ, repaired of bad behavior and its assets. Marriage is moreover replicated and made new in Christ. Jesus tells us that in the Kingdom of God the very tough relationship of a couple that God at first expected can again be grasped (see Matthew 19:6-11). By the excellence of the Holy Spirit, wedded couples can now truly appreciate and regard one another. St. Paul tells us that marriage exhibits the veracity of the steady love of Christ for his Church. Along these lines, mates should love their spouses, "even as Christ revered the gathering and gave himself over for her to favor her" (Ephesians

5:25-26). Mates, too, are called to revere their spouses as the Church loves Christ (see Ephesians 5:22-23). Once more the Old Testament also shows how God prepared his family to adore the association of marriage. God's concurrence with his family was an image of the particular and committed love of a couple. The prophets helped people by seeing that God had not arranged for a couple to be confined (See Hosea 1-3; Isaiah 54 and 62; Jeremiah 2-3 and 31; Ezekiel 16 and 23; Malachi 2:13-17). The books of Ruth and Tobit stand up concerning faithfulness and delicacy inside marriage. The Song of Solomon shows how the love for a man and a woman mirrors God's fondness for his family.

Since marriage is put inside the saving mystery of Jesus Christ, Catholics recollect it as a blessed recognition. It is a strategy through which wedded couples fill in warmth for one another and their children, become favored, and get never-ending life.

God's inspiration and intention for marriage. After God made the earth and the animals, He said, "Let Us make man in Our image, according to Our likeness; and let them rule over the fish of the sea and the birds of the sky and the dairy cows and all the earth, and over each slithering thing that hauls on the earth." The record continues, "God made man in His image, in the image of God He made him; male and female He made them" (Genesis 1:26-27).

God's most paramount justification for making man and woman and obliging them in marriage was for the following reasons:

Reason One: mirror His image in the world. Center your thought around those words, and mirror His image. The Hebrew word for "reflect" means to reflect God, to enhance, amplify, and observe Him. Your marriage should reflect God's image to a world that wildly needs to see what His character is. Since we're made in the image of God, people who wouldn't regardless comprehend what God is like should have the choice to look at us and get an impression.

Reason Two: Complete each other and experience fellowship. The hallowed text approaches a second justification behind marriage: to generally complete each other. That is the explanation God said, "It isn't perfect for the man to be isolated from every other person; I will make him an accomplice sensible for him" (Genesis 2:18).

Adam felt isolated in the nursery, consequently, God made woman clear out his aloneness. Staying in contact with the first-century church in Corinth, Paul rehashed the illustrations in Genesis 2 when he confirmed, "In any case, in the Lord, nor is woman liberated from man, nor is man independent of woman" (1 Corinthians 11:11).

Reason Three: Multiply a certified legacy. A line of certified family members – your youths – will pass an impression of God's character on to what's in store. Your game plans for youngsters could regardless be from this point forward, but if He gives you a youngster, you will be in for a surprising encounter.

God's extraordinary game plan expected the home to be a sort of nursery – a supporting spot where youths grow up to learn character, values, and decency. An inordinate number of couples today have all the earmarks of raising their young people without a sensation of mission and course. They aren't giving to them the meaning of leaving a significant practice of changed lives. They aren't surveying their lives thinking about the Great Commission of Matthew 28:18-20, where Christ orders us to show the gospel to all nations.

One of your errands is to concede a sensation of destiny, a significant mission, to your children. Your commitment as a group is to cause your home where your children acknowledge cherishing and conform to God. Your home should be an educational center to set up your children to look at the prerequisites of people and the world through the eyes of Jesus Christ. If kids don't embrace this significant mission as they grow up, they could continue with their entire lives without experiencing the distinction of God including them in a basic way.

Your marriage is more huge than you could have any time imagined because it impacts God's remaining on this planet. That is the explanation it's key for you to isolate Jesus Christ as the Builder of your home.

Chapter Two

STAGES IN THE JOURNEY OF MARRIAGE

1. **Recognizable proof and Decision:**

God doesn't allow His own an opportunity or permit them to look for their better half or spouse.

His own are the individuals who genuinely submit to Him yet acknowledge He doesn't compel Himself to you; God generally allows man to pick his/her way. After Adam understood that he wanted a partner, God didn't tell Adam to search, go get.

If Adam was permitted to find, what might he at some point emerge with as an assistant, an accomplice, a friend? A primate, a monkey, a gorilla, a cow, a goat; straight a creature.

At the point when you go out to look for a partner, a friend, an accomplice, spouse, or wife, without permitting God to make one for you, you emerge with a creature.

Many individuals even Christians have ignored God's reason relationships are not relationships since we have gone out to look, emerged with a creature, and wedded a creature.

God brings the ideal match He has made to you.

You simply need to rest and your Godly Heavenly made wonderful spouse or wife will be brought to you with perfect timing and spot. Happen with your life like there isn't anything you want, as you don't want to.

Center around God and He will bring the ideal accomplice He has made for you brilliantly and when you will see her/him at the initial time, similar to Adam you will say, 'This is currently bone of my bones, and tissue of my tissue: she will be called Woman since she was removed from Man (Gen 2:23)'.

Indeed! Whenever God first presents your partner to you, you will see him/her and unquestionably know and say, 'that is she or he'. S/he is my bone of bones and tissue of my tissue'. My significant other or my better half.

Individuals who have stayed with God and submitted to Him, have found their God-made accomplices. Inquire as to whether they understood whenever they first saw one another if s/he was the one. The response is Yes!

Hang tight for God, you can pause!

Subsequently, individual Christians and each individual who will run over this instruction, figure out how to submit to God. Rest and trust that God will make and bring your ideal accomplice with perfect timing and spot. He will do it with impeccable timing.

Going out to look or find a spouse or wife is conflicting with God's plan of creation; making you.

2. **Relationship**:

As per me, a genuine relationship is between two defective creatures including one preeminent being. The love ought to resemble a triangle where Christ is at the top importance Christ is the source and the man and lady are getting close underneath the two corners meaning the two of them are beneficiaries of the adoration for Christ.

Before the couple starts to cherish each other, they should initially get love from Christ who is the source. The just way a man can completely adore a lady as per the scriptural perspective, which states that a man ought to adore his better half similarly as Christ adored the church, is assuming the man initially gets love from Christ the wellspring of adoration.

Jeremiah 31:3 says that Christ has cherished us with a never-ending love. The extreme evidence of this was exhibited on the cross. christ is love since he is proof of God's adoration for us. God utilized Christ to show his affection for us.
Consequently, a couple ought to shift focus over to Christ to know how to cherish one another.

Since a genuine relationship includes two creatures and Christ, a brought-back-to-life Christian can't enter a relationship with a non-believer. The Bible orders us not to be conjoined with nonbelievers for what organization does light have with obscurity?

The strategy of building a healthy Christian relationship with your partner before marriage is two-facet. Being a Christian and building a healthy relationship.

Achieving these Christian dating goals requires a high level of commitment from couples.

Unlike worldly dating where everything goes, there are a lot of biblical dating boundaries for Christian couples.

The scripture tells us in Timothy 2:22 to flee from youthful passions and pursue righteousness. The guidelines of a godly relationship are in line with the scripture. Letting God guide your relationship is a necessary commitment for a God-centered relationship.

You do not have to conform to worldly standards during the period of your courtship. You need to be resolute to structure your courtship style to be the acceptable will of God.

Chapter Three

WEDDING

A congregation is far beyond just a setting for your wedding. Novel and unique things become a piece of your marriage, on an actual day and then some:

A congregation wedding will add a profound aspect to your marriage. The service incorporates God and seeks him for help and direction. God's favoring is the fundamental fascination for some couples, whatever their convictions.
You can commit astounding promises, or commitments, in a congregation. You can sincerely commit to promises this large in a congregation. These commitments, made out in the open, will assist you with remaining together and becoming together.

God and your congregation are there for you to assist you with keeping

The Vicar plays an extremely specific part to play in your wedding. They can mix old customs and current experiences to mirror your story. Given the relationship with the Vicar, your wedding can be made individual, noteworthy, significant, and wonderful.
Church structures offer remarkable excellence. Old or new, private or terrific, our 16,000 houses of worship are a portion of the country's most shocking wedding settings, with 66% being recorded structures.
Church structures offer hundreds of years of history. Envision every one of the couples who have hitched in your nearby church, some of whom likely could be your loved ones. You can feel you're turning out to be essential for history itself, the greater arrangement, by a wedding in a similar spot as your family members. We realize such

associations can fill your heart with joy significantly more extraordinary.

You can be associated with pursuing decisions about your function. You could utilize our internet-based function organizer to kick you off.

For certain individuals, a congregation seems like the legitimate spot to get hitched. Chapels can be depicted as 'quiet', 'peaceful', or having an environment that makes a wedding there an especially extraordinary encounter.

Furthermore, after your wedding, you'll understand that a congregation is more than just a wedding setting. We'll continuously be hanging around for you.

Chapter Four

MARRIAGE

We hear a great deal about Christian relationships being unique, yet would it be that makes a marriage "Christian"?

A decent marriage would be between a visually impaired spouse and a hard-of-hearing husband.
Marriage has gotten a seriously terrible standing throughout the long term. The butt of a boundless number of jokes, marriage is a wellspring of interminable social editorial, orientation governmental issues, and legislative discussion.

Love: A transitory craziness treatable by marriage.

In the United States, marriage has fallen upon especially tough situations. Increasingly few individuals are deciding to marry, as a matter of fact, not exactly 50% of current US families are comprised of hitched couples. The level of Americans who have never hitched is growing while the quantity of couples living respectively without a wedding is expanding exponentially. Meanwhile, an ever-increasing number of kids are destined to be single mothers.

One ought to continuously be enamored. That is the explanation one ought to never marry.

To top everything off, America has the most elevated separate rate among Western countries and the most elevated occurrence of single-parent groups of any industrialized nation. There's no rejecting that the scene of the American family has changed profoundly throughout recent years.

Marriage and culture :

These measurements bring up issues about the worth and importance of marriage in contemporary American culture. Given changes in conceptive innovation, changes in social perspectives about sexual ethical quality, and the clear disappointment of marriage as an optimal relationship, has marriage become immaterial?

However it could appear in this way, that sociologists Mark Regnerus and Jeremy Uecker as of late announced that the American youth are as keen on marriage as whenever — over 95% expect to wed someday.

In any case, from romance books to unscripted television to motion pictures, unreasonable assumptions and misleading understandings about adoration, marriage, and sentiment are handily propagated.

Thus, both those searching out a marriage accomplice and those attempting to remain in a marriage battle with errors in the meaning of that relationship itself.

Could the Christian confidence at any point affect this comprehension and the mission for a significant marriage?

Marriage and faith:
However marriage isn't the particular space of the Christian church, the Bible and powerful Christian masterminds truly do have a lot to say on the matter. So what makes a marriage a Christian marriage?

Just being strict or purporting Christian convictions isn't a fix-all; it doesn't ensure a durable, ecstatic marriage. To address our inquiries, we should take a gander at the fundamental components of Christian marriage and perceive how they contrast with different ways to deal with the marriage.

As soon as the primary hundred years, Christian journalists have remarked on the connection between their confidence and marriage. One essayist, Paul, wrote these words:

Spouses should adore their wives as their bodies. He who cherishes his better half loves himself. All things considered, nobody at any point abhorred their own body, however, they feed and care for their body, similarly to the congregation – for we are individuals from his body. "Hence a man will leave his dad and mom and be joined to his significant other, and the two will become one tissue." This is a significant secret – however, I am discussing Christ and the congregation. In any case, every last one of you likewise should adore his significant other as he cherishes himself, and the spouse should regard her husband.

In these refrains, Paul thinks about the connection between a couple to the connection between Jesus and the congregation. This has staggeringly significant ramifications for the idea of Christian marriage.

The covenant of marriage:
Christians approach marriage as a contract, a relationship given commitments and responsibility, not simply sentiments – however, love is unquestionably involved.

The idea of marriage as a contract is established in the Hebrew confidence, and early Christians saved the conviction as well. God's pledge with Israel was established on his guarantee to be dedicated to Israel. The Hebrew public guaranteed dependability to God also, however, the Bible doesn't conceal that they battled – and frequently fizzled – to keep that promise. Like God with the

Israelites, Jesus laid out what he called "another agreement" with his followers.16

To discuss marriage as a pledge is to say that the accomplices make common commitments about how they will decide to live from here on out, not only statements of how they feel in the present. The undertaking to live into those commitments — staying dedicated to their agreement — will shape their characters throughout the long term.

Christian love:

Christian marriage is likewise particularly founded on agapē, the Greek word utilized in Jesus' lessons and early Christian compositions to depict the sort of adoration God communicates to people. Agapē doesn't have anything to do with the whimsical ideas of heartfelt love whereupon so many American social marriage fantasies are established.

Despite how pleasurable such sentiments might be at the start of a relationship, they only occasionally have the resilience to endure a long period of high points and low points — the "for better or in negative ways" of matrimony.

Agapē is a unique idea, so vital that Paul committed an entire part of his most memorable letter to the Corinthians to characterizing it. You might have heard a notable expression from this segment: "Love shows restraint, love is benevolent." Paul then proceeds to depict a conciliatory approach to cherishing others.

This sort of unqualified love — or a functioning endeavoring to experience this sort of adoration every day — marks a truly Christian marriage, similarly, as it portrays a legitimately Christian life.19 is tracked down in a functioning decision one makes about how to act toward another, not a restrictive inclination one has toward someone.20Agapē depends on the purposeful options of the darling, not the reactions of the cherished.

Christ-centered marriage:

Maybe the most unmistakable attribute of Christian marriage – which makes the other two potential – is that it is purposefully fixated on Jesus Christ. Every mate consistently attempts to be aware, love, and comply with Jesus, and follow his model.

Along these lines, a couple of figure out how to communicate Agapē and stay devoted to their pledge. As they practice the Christian confidence together, they push toward one another, filling together infatuated and solidarity.

Yet, what might be said about a marriage in which only one life partner is a devotee of Jesus? At any point might that marriage at any point be a "Christian marriage"?

Paul expounds on such a case in 1 Corinthians 7:12-16.21 He encourages the trusting accomplice to remain wedded to their unbelieving companion due to the devotee's effect on their accomplice and youngsters. One individual who is looking to follow Jesus Christ, figuring out how to live out of Agapē, and keeping the commitments of the agreement carries Christ's presence into the marriage.

Consistent pursuit:

Christian or not, marriage is hard for any couple to support over a long period. Life's preliminaries — the tension of earning enough to pay the bills, of nurturing, of opposing compulsions to faithlessness or self-centeredness — can strain any marriage.

Be that as it may, Christian marriage offers trust. The expectation is that a couple, by deliberately deciding to figure out how to cherish dependably and conciliatorily as

Jesus did, may keep their contract guarantees for a lifetime.

Chapter Five

HOME MANAGEMENT

Home discussions of where a man and a lady live respectively as a couple having consolidated in heavenly marriage. It is God's foundation all along - Gen. 2:18; 21-24; Matt> 19:4-6. A home can be a genuine one or a wicked one relying upon who is in - charge, the one in charge, and the one deciding and coordinating the undertakings of the home. Where Jesus is in - charge, then, it will be a faithful home. Everything will be finished in the anxiety toward God. The executives with the end goal of our conversation here simply running. Home administration thusly, implies how Christians ought to run their homes.

HOW CHRISTIANS SHOULD RUN THEIR HOMES

They ought to run their homes as indicated by the Word of God-Eph. 5:21-25.

-Both the spouse and the wife ought to regard each other Eph. 5:21.

-The spouse should submit to her significant other irrefutably Eph. 5:22, 24; 1 Pet. 3:1

This celebrated God - Col. 3:18

-The spouse ought to exhibit unrestricted love for his significant other. He is to start endowments instead of fight back when things turn out badly very much like Christ did - Eph. 5:25. All together that their requests may be replied by God unhindered, men ought to cherish and respects their spouses - 1 Pet. 3:7.

The man ought to be the Priest of home - Eph. 5:23. He is to hear from God, lead his home in the love of God and convey family petitions to God, lead his home in the love of God and plan for the family. He is likewise to caution them when inconvenience is seen.

Parents ought to show their kids the expression of God. Never abandon them with the assistance of God and show them the method of God right off the bat throughout everyday life - Eph. 6:4; Deut. 6:6-7;

Prov. 22:6; 1 Tim. 1:3-5

Permit God to be in - charge of your home and afterward, your home will give joy to your Maker and you will be a good example to other people.

Chapter Six

HUSBAND'S RESPONSIBILITIES IN MARRIAGE

the off chance that the Lord has given you a spouse, He calls you to cherish her, grasp her, respect her, lead her, accommodate her, and lay down with her.

Love her

"Spouses, love your wives, as Christ adored the congregation and surrendered himself for her" (Ephesians 5:25). Christ's adoration for His congregation went up to this point that He was ready beyond words. Similarly, spouses ought to adore their wives much a lot that they will give their lives for them. No one can cherish like Jesus adored, so arriving at the standard that the Bible gives us is incomprehensible. This ought to cause each spouse to acknowledge he wants to rely upon the Lord day to day to adore his better half however much he ought to.

Figure out here
"Spouses, live with your wives in a seeing way" (1 Peter 3:7). However numerous men think it is difficult to figure out ladies, if you are a spouse you are called to give your all to grasp no less than one: your better half. You need to pay attention to her. You need to pose her inquiries. You need to understand that her sentiments work uniquely in contrast to your sentiments.

Honor her
"Showing distinction to the lady as the more vulnerable vessel" (1 Peter 3:7). Since both

you and your better half have a spirit forever, you have equivalent worth. Since your significant other is more fragile than you will be, you want to respect her extraordinarily to show you understand her value. You additionally need to safeguard her. Woman's rights demand clouding contrasts among people. This prompts a deficiency of the acknowledgment that men need to respect and safeguard ladies, particularly spouses and their wives. In the drudgery of everyday living, the order of spouses to "not be unforgiving" with their wives (Colossians 3:19) is one of the main ways of showing the honor of wives' merit.

Lead her

"The spouse is the top of the wife even as Christ is the top of the congregation" (Ephesians 5:23). In marriage, a couple each plays their part and obligation. Here we see that a blissful marriage is a marriage where a spouse gives cherishing initiative to his better half, looking for the best for herself and their loved ones.

Accommodate her

A spouse ought to feed and value his better half (Ephesians 5:29). He ensures that food and sanctuary are given, both actually and profoundly.

Lay down with her

"The spouse ought to provide for his better half her intimate privileges" (1 Corinthians 7:3). This stanza shows that even in sexual connections, the spouse is giving, not taking. His accentuation is for his significant other's pleasure, not his own. Sexuality is commended in the Bible (see Song of Songs, Proverbs 5). It is to be delighted inside the boundaries that God has set for it - the marriage of a man and a lady. A spouse is called to be generally dedicated to his significant other (Hebrews 13:4).

Having a spouse is a gift from the Lord (Proverbs 18:22). Assuming you have gotten that gift, honor God and honor your significant other by getting her concurring God's rules

Chapter Seven

WIFE'S RESPONSIBILITIES IN MARRIAGE

A wife's responsibilities may be more than at some other time ever, ladies today need an unmistakable comprehension of how they ought to connect with their spouses. The critical social changes achieved by the ladies' freedom development throughout recent many years have prompted such disarray that the general concept of "jobs" is repulsive to some. They feel as though some way or another they lose their character and their opportunity if they stick to some sort of "obsolete norm."

We must check out plainly what the Bible says regarding this matter. And keeping in mind that the Bible doesn't matter our cutting edge word "job" to marriage, the Scriptures are clear about the special obligations God relegates to a spouse. Unique note: I propose that you additionally read Dennis' response to the inquiry, "What ought to be the spouse's job in marriage?" before you proceed with this segment. A spouse's liabilities can be appropriately seen exclusively with regards to cherishing, worker initiative by her significant other.

1. Be a partner to your significant other.

While we all are called to be partners to other people, the Bible puts an extraordinary accentuation on this obligation regarding spouses. The beginning lets us know that God acknowledged it wasn't great for man to be distant from everyone else, and that He chose to make a "partner reasonable for him" (Gen. 2:18). It is fascinating to take note of the Hebrew significance of the word partner in this entry is found from now on in the Bible to allude just to God as He helps us. The way that this equivalent word is applied to a spouse implies that we ladies have been given colossal power for good in our husbands' lives. God has planned spouses to assist their husbands with turning into all that God means for them to be.

2. Regard your significant other.

In Ephesians 5:33, Paul says, " ... the spouse should regard her significant other." When you regard your better half you respect him, notice him, respect him, honor him, lean toward him, and regard him. It implies esteeming his perspective, respecting his insight and character, appreciating his obligation to you, and taking into account his requirements and values. Our spouses have some requirements. The macho man who is independent, free, and immune is a legend. On one occasion Dennis provided me with a rundown of what he viewed as a portion of the essential requirements most men have:

Fearlessness in his personhood as a man

To be paid attention to

Friendship

To be required

Addressing these requirements regarding your better half is about. To reinforce Dennis' certainty, for instance, I attempt to empower him by being his main fan. Each spouse maintains that his significant other should be in his group, to mentor him when important, however in particular to be his team promoter. A spouse needs a wife who is behind him, putting stock in him, appreciating him, and giving a shout-out to him as he goes out into the world consistently.

3. Love your better half.

Titus 2:4 calls for spouses "to cherish their husbands." A decent depiction of the sort of adoration your better half requirements is "unqualified acknowledgment." at the end of the day, acknowledge your significant other similarly as he is – a defective individual. Love likewise implies being focused on a commonly satisfying sexual relationship. I understand there is significantly more to adore than sex, yet we are taking a gander at how to satisfy God's order to cherish our spouses. Along these lines, we should take a gander at affection according to their viewpoint, in addition to our own. Reviews show that sex is one of a man's most significant necessities – if not the most significant. At the point when a spouse opposes closeness, is uninterested, or is just latently intrigued, her significant other may feel dismissed It will cut at his mental self-view, tear at him to the actual focus of his being, and make detachment. My significant other's sexual necessities ought to be more significant and higher on my need list than menus, housework, ventures, exercises, and, surprisingly, the youngsters. It doesn't imply that I ought to ponder sex the entire day and consistently, however it implies that I track down ways of recalling my significant other and his necessities. It implies I save a portion of my energy for him. This holds me back from being self-centered and living just for my requirements and needs. Keeping up with that center assists me with overcoming detachment in our marriage.

4. Submit to the authority of your significant other.

Simply notice "accommodation," and numerous ladies promptly become upset and, surprisingly, threatening. A few married couples accept accommodation and the ladies are mediocre compared to men here and there. That's what a few ladies believe if they submit they will lose their personality and become non-people. Others dread (some not surprisingly) that accommodation prompts are utilized or mishandled. Another misinterpretation is that accommodation implies blind dutifulness concerning the lady. She can give no contribution to her better half, question nothing, and just stay respectfully shoeless and pregnant in the kitchen. What would God have in care? Here is a vital entry from Scripture:

Spouses, be dependent upon your husbands, regarding the Lord. For the spouse is the top of the wife, as Christ additionally is the top of the congregation, He being the Savior of the body. Yet, as the congregation is dependent upon Christ, so additionally the spouses should be to their husbands in all things. Spouses, love your wives, similarly, as Christ additionally cherished the congregation and surrendered Himself for her, so He could purify her, having purged her by the washing of water with the word, that He could present to Himself the congregation in the entirety of her brilliance, having no spot or flaw or anything like that; however that she would be blessed and exemplary. So spouses should likewise cherish their wives as their bodies. He who adores his own better half loves himself; for nobody at any point detested his tissue, however, feeds and appreciates it, similarly as Christ additionally does the congregation, since we are individuals from His body. — Ephesians 5:22-30

Chapter Eight

CHILDREN UPBRINGING

This 21st century is most certainly an impacting world and nurturing must be deliberate. Presently with regards to bringing up Godly kids, it takes cautious thought particularly as it won't simply work out. Profound Parenting is about your job as a profoundly disapproved parent; the natural job that is yours alone. The following are a few hints about Godly nurturing:

1. Youngsters ought to be educated to be positive about themselves:

Each youngster is one of a kind and ought to be educated so. They are different with innate qualities, gifts, and abilities. Keep away from correlations among kids and cruel analysis. Accordingly instructing them that God loves them thus so you.

2. Train them to esteem others:

Surprisingly understanding that they are novel, they ought to likewise figure out how to regard and esteem others independent of their status throughout everyday life. Tell them that they are advantaged. Furthermore, instruct them that with those honors come liability and they should be conscious.

3. Instruct them that they are called to lead and not to follow:

Help them that it is OK to say NO and to appear as something else. They ought to be prepared to be certain of administration. They ought to represent what they have confidence in. As guardians, we ought to guarantee that what they put stock in mirrors the standards of HONESTY and INTEGRITY. Instruct them that genuine pioneers additionally serve individuals.

4. Put down stopping points from the get-go in their lives:

Kids' freedom ought to be expanded based on their awareness of others' expectations. Suitable compensations for excellent obligations will likewise empower a youngster. A kid who gets all that the individual needs will more often than not grow up with a negative penchant for selfishness. Help them to have defined limits. Setting up a severe sleep time routine is one such model that should be followed come what may. Go through this Sleep Blog to find solid rest tips for your youngster. They ought to be instructed to believe in God who gives and appeal to their requirements.

5. Discipline (Punitive and Non-Punitive):

Do whatever it takes not to teach out of frustration. Likewise, don't convey void intimidations. There ought to be a fair way to deal with discipline. For example, as a youngster becomes older, guardians ought to figure out how to impart/reason more and rebuff less.

The discipline ought to be proportionate to the bad behavior. Discipline ought to be steady and guardians shouldn't convey contradictory signals. At the point when done right sure discipline ought to make closeness and not distance. In such circumstances, the kid knows to return and apologize.

6. Keep the Lines of Communication open:

While conversing with your kids, don't be frightened at anything you hear. Try not to be critical, keep a receptive outlook. Keep mentally collected and offer viable responses however much as could be expected. Additionally, know the loved ones of their companions. Whenever they feel happy with conversing with you, then, at that point, you can point them in the correct course piously.

7. Construct a protected town around them:

It takes a town to bring up a kid. Show them how to stay away from improper contact with anybody and to make some noise assuming it at any point works out. Tell them that their bodies are theirs and that their body is a sanctuary of God.

8. Model what you maintain that they should learn:

Try not to be unique about what you are attempting to educate them about. This is because kids will quite often reflect on what they see, instead of standing by listening to everything you say to them. So guardians must walk through your discussion. To bring up genuine kids, you should display the right qualities. Above all, let them see you supplicate, and gain what love is from how you treat individuals

www.ingramcontent.com/pod-product-compliance
Lightning Source LLC
LaVergne TN
LVHW020524160826
845677LV00015B/3885